Spiritual Necessity

ALSO AVAILABLE FROM STATION HILL

Frank Samperi, *LETARGO*

Spiritual Necessity

selected poems of
Frank Samperi

edited by
John Martone

BARRYTOWN
STATION HILL

Published by Barrytown/Station Hill Press, Inc., Barrytown, NY, 12507, as a project of the Institute for Publishing Arts, Inc., in Barrytown, New York, a not-for-profit, tax-exempt organization [501(c)(3)], supported in part by grants from the New York State Council on the Arts.

Cover design by Susan Quasha
Typeset by Chie Hasegawa and Kate Schapira

Library of Congress Cataloging-in-Publication Data

Samperi, Frank.
  Spiritual necessity : selected poems of Frank Samperi / John Martone, editor.
      p. cm.
  ISBN 158177088X
  I. Martone, John, 1952- II. Title.

PS3569.A466A6 2003
811'.54—dc21

                              2002155811

Contents

Introduction

As a poet, as in other respects, Frank Samperi stood apart. Orphan and first generation Italian-American, he discovered Dante in a Brooklyn institution, taught himself Aquinas in Latin, studied the Indian philosopher Sankara, non-Euclidean geometry, and astrology. Although his poetic idiom remains thoroughly contemporary, Samperi was in many respects a medieval Catholic visionary trying to find his way in a deeply troubled America, the vacuous materialism and superficiality of which he could not abide. As a consequence, his work was not just counter-cultural but also counter-fashionable. Although discovered by Louis Zukofsky and Cid Corman, and appreciated by other poets of his generation, including Robert Creeley, Robert Kelly, and Will Petersen, as well as other "knowing readers," Samperi's poetry has heretofore been available only in limited editions. This collection hopes to make his work more readily available to a new and wider audience.

Samperi was one of that vital generation for whom poetry and life were a single task. Along with Olson's *Maximus Poems*, Larry Eigner's countless books, and Corman's *Of,* Samperi's work belongs to that distinctively American genre of the *life-poem*. His work is a radical autobiography, structured upon image rather narrative. Fidelity to perception and economy of means are central to this poetic, and many poems in *The Prefiguration* are studies of American fact in the objectivist manner:

>   the
>   trains
>
>   shaking
>   the
>   dust

from
the
El

scatter
the
birds

from
the
trees

to
the
roofs

 Poet of everyday life, Samperi, is also on a visionary pilgrimage, and here his chief model is Dante. The centerpiece of Samperi's life-poem—and second volume of the trilogy which also includes *The Prefiguration* and *Lumen Gloriae*—is *Quadrifariam*, the title of which refers to the four-fold allegory of Dante's *Commedia*. Samperi's allegory, however, reflects his own cultural moment. American life is disjointed, and Samperi must illuminate that disjointedness, if he is to make progress on his pilgrimage, if he is to get anywhere else. Allegory is "broken" in this poetic universe. In contrast to Dante's world, where we always know where we are, we feel constantly dis/located in Samperi's. We have not 100 cantos arranged symmetrically, but more than a thousand poems arranged in sequences and tangential movements that intimate the great circle. By shifting of our frame of reference (from the details of daily life, to dream imagery, to social critique, to the philosophical debát) Samperi creates an American work that is about never being at home in America, a poetry of contemporary spiritual homelessness.

 Samperi's alterity is key to his vision. With his orphan past, he belongs nowhere and to no one. He is also deeply committed to the Dantean heritage, with its theme of the exile poet, the *homo viator*. These make him that which is perhaps most outcast in American culture: an original. Samperi's pilgrimage is a search for origins, but it widens instead of simply coming full circle. Samperi may hope to recover "anterior time" but he knows that "transformation/prevent[s]/return." In late poems, such as this piece from *Letargo*, he becomes explicitly, even courageously ec/centric and anti-closural:

> *give over, then, go daily*

> tired of the world,
> creation also
> seems far
> fetched:

> voice
> voiceless speaking
> not the
> same

His project reconciles the interior vision of Dante and the objectivist fact of American poetry in light of Zukofsky and Williams. It could perhaps only have been realized by Samperi, cut off from his roots in Italy, on the one hand, and alienated from the poetic avant-garde on the other. Paradoxically, his orphan work can boast a complex and rich parentage.

Editing Samperi's work presents specific challenges. On the one hand, he wrote but one long poem with structural complexities reminiscent of Dante's *Commedia*, complete with late-twentieth century versions of his predecessor's canticles, cantos and episodes. Each of Samperi's volumes is in fact a poetic sequence made up of subsequences, which are sometimes named, sometimes partitioned by blank pages. Conveying a sense of the individual lyric in its own right and in terms of its place in the opus is a difficult proposition in a volume of selected poems. The meditative and visual qualities of Samperi's work also require abundant "white space" in any faithful edition.

This text respects the idiosyncracies of punctuation and orthography of the original editions. To the extent possible, I have tried to limn the architecture of Samperi's work by representing not just every book, but where possible, all the sequences within each volume. There are—inevitably—gaps, but hopefully this selection will suggest to the reader the scope and depth of Samperi's vision.

JOHN MARTONE
Huntington, NY, 2003

Preface

Frank Samperi was legendary for the purity of his poetry. His language was clear the way glass is, demanding only attention to its luster, and to the world it lets through. His poems are statements, clean as rock crystal, rhythmically minimal, intellectually ardent.

Samperi responded to urban contradiction by erasure. His work is built of silences hard won from the crapulous tumult of Lower East Side nights in Manhattan where his great years of work were spent. I think of him sitting there, night after night, as he described it in his delicate letters to me, letters carefully handwritten in ink, on pages neatly folded as had been *comme il faut* in our childhoods—page one, page three, page two, page four is how it ran.

He used the word *study* to identify this night labor of his. While the rest of us were experimenting among the nocturnals with passions and potions, he was studying his masters. Aristotle, Aquinas, Shankara the acharya he spoke of as his masters, and Dante, closest of all. He wrote from among their company, not as a modern going back for insight and system, but as one of their contemporaries, perhaps one of Dante's *fideli d'amore* about whom we corresponded much, Love's Faithful Ones who had learned—it seems to me from Ibn al-Arabi and the Sufis—an order of intellection grounded in the ardor of real love and its articulations.

In that sense, for all the chastity and austerity (quite a different quality) of his work, he is a love poet. Since it is love, as Augustine says, which summons us to the things of this world. Even the tumult outside his window, the shrill of art in the making, the street our mother—he held those things too in his regard, and spoke of them quietly, his usually short lines lying like cross-streets along the avenues of silence.

His are poems that insist so much on their own quietness that they finally, nun-like, live in black and white, shaming us to pay attention. It is attention they never particularly got in his lifetime—and I must say that in none of his letters to me, and the rare phone calls, and the single visit we shared, did he ever complain with melancholy, let alone bitterness, about the neglect he might well have bemoaned. Many a poet who got vastly more public attention than Samperi ever got has been plaintive or vitriolic about perceived neglect. For Samperi, as long as he was paying attention to the words, that was attention enough.

I'm very glad, though, that people are waking up to his work now.

ROBERT KELLY
January 2003

Spiritual Necessity

The Prefiguration (1971)

On the night of my death
fires will lace
the shoreline
of some unknown beach—

and children
        in loose
            half-length
      blue gowns
will sing my dirge
as unknown vagrants
place my body
on a raft

        covered with lilies
        and seaweed—

and after they have
fastened down my body
with rope
      they (the vagrants)
and the children
will set
           the raft
    adrift

I am an anchorite.
        and (I am Manfred's half-brother.)

In the morning
I go to a coffee shop.

        Sunlight is
        on things.

the young wives are wheeling baby carriages
the old wives are carrying large packages of food

        The Avenue
        seethes with health.

After I have had
my coffee and toast
I go back to my furnished room.

        I am stirred by some
        white blossoms near
        low uncut hedges.
        and

the wind cools my eyes—
for the trees are blinding.

In a moment
I shall be in the room
and I shall be glad.

        I cannot bear
        sunlight in the morning.

I waste

       my afternoons
       in streets

where faces

       drift

in sunlight

       and brick homes

fling

       Mozart tunes

against Pet shops.

       Damn it,

there's something

       wrong

with this place,

       says an old man,

as I wait for a bus.

Hapless, I shall take
my little bag of necessities and move closer
toward the ivory gate—
                              for I have paid
my debts, and having neither father nor
mother nor brother nor sister, I am now granted
freedom—which is the quickest way to death.
But I swear I shall die happy.

To be saved I must
slip away from the moderns

                              quietly

and go to that land
I have heard

            so much
            about (the north wind

the gardens
full
with my favorite
lilacs.

A crowd
stood

in front
o f

the church
gap-

ing as
four

pallbear-
ers

carried
the

coffin
down

the steps
to

the hearse
as

the grieved
chil-

dren of
the

deceased
were

singly
es-

corted
to

the fami-
i-

ly car—

after
when

the last
car

was seen
slow-

ly turn-
ing

around
the

corner
they

went their
way.

A grotto
  A wonder
Of workmanship

Where a bird
  On the shoulder
Of a saint

Sings
  Of a night's
Calvary.

I have seen him
in the garden
when a songbird
blew among bright
branches and a dog
barked in the street,
walk by a rose bush
and along a path of tulips
toward her grave,
which lies to the right
of an apple-tree,
and place a wreath
of white carnations
on the headstone.

This I have seen
him do many times.

My songs
would

praise
her doves;

but now shadows
pass

over
a wall—

and the broken
head

of a Cupid

lies
beside

a cobbled
walk

past
a hothouse.

Our
vines
burn
on

the
garden
wall—
also,

snow
lightly
covers
the

shovel
by
the
wooden
steps.

a dream
  a falling away
  into darkness

after wandering thru
  the wood
  coming out

standing on the edge
  looking down
  the slope

the church
  to the right
  behind pine trees

the playground
  to the left
  behind the school

slanting up
  more pine trees
  on top

arranged in rows
  against the sky
  behind the fence

... must
you talk

of failure;

even this
snow's

right

—ah, oak,
branching

over
my work

shed

after snow
forsythia
bloom against
a white fence

no luck left
only
a memory
of a child

behind
his
attic
window

in memory

the old
men stand
outside
the fence

near the
grape arbor
of the small
two family

house

An old lady
        behind
some artificial
    flowers looks

from her dirty
        ground
floor window
    at the kids

in the school
        yard
a block up
    from the

repair shop
        for the
city's
    buses.

below
levels
o f
hills
white
horses
galloping
down
the
road
from
the
wood
above
the
valley
at
the
foot
o f
the
range
o f
mountains
in
moonlight
against
star

the

    garden's

paths

    darken

under

    plum

blossoms

    in

shadows

    from

the

    walls

going out
to
    the backyard
to shovel snow

away from
the
    cellar door
an old man

looked up
at
    a shadeless
window

blinding
in
    the sun
setting

behind the
homes
    beyond
the freight yard

the

trains

shaking

the

dust

from

the

El

scatter

the

birds

from

the

trees

to

the

roofs

a

branch

in

bloom

in

the

light

from

the

hills

trembles

under

the

lighting

of

birds

hills

behind

the

branches'

shadows

up

past

a

fountain

slope

toward

light

upward

in

    light

flame

in

flame

    dying

to

its

memory

    of

snow

And so
    the bird
was

said
    to rise
from

cinders—
    a way
o f

holding
    the sun
to

heart.

Claudia,
Autumn's
come round
again—

now
leaves
like birds
tumble

from
the hill
behind
our

garden
overlooking
grass sloping
toward

sea.

looking
toward
the
wooded

hill
under
moonlight
you

spoke
o f
the
rose

leaves
o f
our
marriage

day

this crisis
of our life
when the stars
mean little

as background

on
  a
bridge

behind
  branches
an

angel—
  a
memory

o f
  sea
a

longing
  for
home

scattered
  by
the

dance

The new man is always the spiritual man.

We, too, conceive of contemplation as the activity that is wholly compatible with His City; therefore, the act poverty that moves us in that direction is in no sense negative. What we are trying to say is this: to live in God is to be contemplative.

It is wrong to think of contemplation as the opposite of activity: that is, contemplation is a prefiguration of the very activity that pertains to the Kingdom of Heaven. It is the State that fosters the idea that contemplation is passive, therefore, more in keeping with the man who doesn't work, or better who won't contribute to the give and take that is the market. From this it is just to ask: what is the meaning of the word activity when the State is Unity. It's obvious: exploitation.

How can we know life when to measure and to name pertain to determinations wholly our own!

Now what is this problem concerning knowledge: that is, is there any? We cannot place it in words; but even to say *that* is to place the statement in the intention rather than in the real: does this bring us before a background ever changing the moment we start to move toward it?

There is knowledge! and it's of the kind that makes a man see the whole world as the work; therefore, to love the work is to be face to face (would it make much difference if you were to say: to see face to face?).

It all amounts to this: if a man is capable of knowing completely, then his companions are the angels.

To say that a man's knowledge is face to face is to say that the vision is never at odds with the life.

A man need not formulate in such a world: that is, where the vision is never at odds with the life truth can never be an approach.

If truth can never be an approach, then what is it?

The beatific vision brings the world face to face with the Truth.

In the meantime, what do we do?

Aquinas says: "Et in rebus quidem corporalibus apparet quod res visa non potest esse in vidente per suam essentiam, sed solum per suam similitudinem; sicut similitudo lapidis est in oculo, per quam fit visio in actu, non autem ipsa substantia lapidis. Si autem esset una et eadem res, quae esset principium visivae virtutis, et quae esset res visa, oporteret videntem ab illa re et virtutem visivam habere, et formam per quam videret."

The hierarchical orders of the Church can only be valid metaphorically; therefore, every movement toward specific difference is the church's movement toward its proper prefiguration.

A man's proper prefiguration is his proper stance.

The ontological is still propositional. There isn't much that you can say about the real except that it is: this makes one walk freely—that is, no system of thought or just plain system can overshadow him: therefore, if the argument is ontological, then any attempt to re-establish the natural is asymptotic.

Blake's argument against the Analytics is an argument against himself: that is, the ontological is still propositional.

To be fair: to argue existentially or ontologically is to argue incorrectly: however, the former at least stresses that knowledge is in the knower according to the mode of the knower, while the latter encloses existence in its insistence that it has grasped essence.

Blake's prophetic books still remain subservient to history—therefore, he places another generation in the position of a justifier of the ways of God to men: that is, another shall write of him in the way he wrote of Milton.

One has the feeling that Blake's final image of the new heaven and the new earth is an entangled image—that is, there's something discontinuous about it.

Now that you've said that Blake has spoken all the old truths, remembering what his argument against another was, release him, and call him friend.

It came to me in sleep: Blake's Four Zoas is an attempt to square the circle; therefore, the indication is ad infinitum.

Blake never released himself from Homer—that is, his battlefield is the Homeric plain.

From such a *plane* you can only get heroic type—that is, our "contentions ... with dominion ... principalities: is still to be at the mercy of the gods.

The old truth is historical truth.

Since the Material Ideal is not out there with the force of nature, then it follow that its mode of being comes from a reasoning that is ontological.

The resolution of the possibility of a spiritual art is: *isn't* is never valid except in relation to thought.

Riemannian space retains the notion of the horizontal in its confrontation with the unbounded.

A mathematical universe is equilibrated when its formulation is complete; therefore, any substantiation that is existentially presupposed is a consequent rather than an antecedent—that is, the latter is apparential.

This argument has nothing to do with existence or non-existence—its concern is this: the possibility of a progressive formulation, that is, every possible temporal relation solved the universe is solved (it is obvious that the statement *the universe is solved* releases the word possible from any meaning).

Is there any meaning in a formula complete enough to represent a universe in the round?

To be drawn into the market only intensifies one's sense of the ambience that impedes; therefore, any science that pretends to have discovered a means to a re-establishment of the natural has, in truth, simply proposed to the mind an end that places the whole populace in a position conducive toward complete service to the State.

The despair: to say *the* world is to give rhetorical definitiveness to *your* world.

It is obvious that the notions *making it on your own* and *being responsible* are there solely for the sake of stressing the eternity in the now.

Linguistics is the sole study of the logomachist.

Looking out only to refer back and then finally looking out significantly.

A doctrine is only valid ontologically, that is, nothing that one man or another can say can place the meaning unequivocally there rather than here. What is intended is a boundary that reduces each man's movement to a movement essential in the sense that the ambience is but a projection of his inner state.

I hear of Ren's
illness—and hope
this concern

finds him
up and around
hungry for cookies

and tea; and ready
for rompings
in snow—not yet?

then, at least,
at the window
watching

his playmates
belly-whopping
down the hills

below Mt. Hiei

l'envoi

Go, song, to Will and Ami;
tell them of my concern; be
graceful in your phrasing
try to speak of melting snow.

here's
a
cherry
spray

for
each
o f
you

—could
n't
find
any

birds;
they've
flown
to

woods

Passing by the shops past the El
past the blossoming
apple-trees
a man
turns down a street
to factories
and then up
to homes
looking toward weeds
along tracks

Quarter
moon
car
turning   corner
rear view
window
five storey
trucking
co.

against light you my wife gather flowers along
the river reflecting hill and forsythia
     at night, your fragrance dissolves metaphor

in the midst of the collapse our room dark our
speech our love the background

our bodies naked given up to each the other reveal
the ecstasy the earth

the world a river flower reflecting light revealing
a river flower the world reveals our love in love

your odor returning night the bed our love returns
sea our first year

body to body our night less boundary than fragrance
releases bird hill river

Quadrifariam (1973)

FROM *THE TRIUNE*

I walked conversing with angels—
trees to the right
animals to the left
the path beyond quiet—
we moved toward the animals—
they moved with us toward flame
the quiet
then the air changed
the right reflected the left
and the movements ceased—
my spirit vanished beyond the hill—
birds flew up from the trees above the river
then night
wind
The creation
close
revealing no trap
man and woman
close
the leaves shading
their movement past water toward hill
Angels above water—
we came down the hill the sun beyond the trees—
we talked with men and women
their light not from themselves
nevertheless radiant the branches glinting
from their nearness—

we continued along the paths
No journey draws significance from the encyclopediac
destitute of references the seeing
gathers to itself always the proper
never once recalling impediment
in love therefore center or edge
meaningless
the sun setting behind us

Taking the path beyond the water
we came to a field
more people
some looked at us
others turned away
the background the sea
we passed lilies climbed the hill to the right
Circle whose center was no where visible except as
circumference presupposed itself as center to a
circumference no where visible
Then turning to the left the sun setting
we walked toward the wood beyond the river
people under a tree were speaking of women and
children wandering in deserts—
continuing along the path
we met a man sitting against a rock
he was blind
he talked only of the ancient world
we knew the stories—
before entering the wood
I could still hear his song
Resolution the hill
the light
nevertheless out of deference
scattered flowers along the paths
then down to the right above water
came to a clearing—
already late morning—
we took the path to the desert
We sat in a garden
a reflection of star mountain leaf
the paths quiet
wind
music
body

No resolution possible
the sentimental gradational
therefore primitive
nor if differential
an opposite
I walked along buildings
up ahead a park and apartments beyond
left and right rivers
the geographical false
stressing a position
a totality as it appears in imagination
this not to say
a totality present
the vision differential
The park quiet
I climbed rocks
came to paths to bridges
to grass trees beyond
turned down to a lake
few rowboats out
some boys their pants rolled up
fishing at the edge
then up to a hill
the path to the street beyond the playground
I came to theaters
the crowds the shops
a complement
in memory
in the grove above the river angels
we passed animals
the odor the grass
we sat on a bank
the sun rising
then to warehouses
the waterfront a block down

We sat on a rock
people passing by a wood
the water reflecting a hill
memory the city
returning the man
the bench
old men drunks
the lovers under a tree
then we walked along the river
turned to the right
the path to a wood
animals tired
groping we came to a clearing
a man and a woman lying amidst grass
to the right mountains
the sun rising
Night
the river quiet
people sorrowing
their words revealing the old
the community
a man bowed near water
the wood above
we came to a hill
implication the reflection
then water reflecting hill
hill no longer implication
Up over rocks to a field
the sea below
then to the right
a ledge to the shore
stars
cliffs
memory
dust

Dying to the contemporary
the walk again
involving rain the vision
the exhaustion unable to resolve itself
the memory
people discussing
alienation
the ambience failing
to fulfill each person differentially
a woman's words
if you spoke to me more often
wind
a slope forsythia
the afternoons
walks for miles
a word one word
if you spoke to me
I wouldn't be so lonely
night
the car lots
better a movie a bar
the return
home the darkness
oak
the chimes
restoring the man
we stood in a park
looking up at
the big clock
my wife
my children
altering the words
the neons skyscrapers
warehouses
past

Death
the memory
shadow
then river
mountain
grove
past
wood recurrence
angel
leaf
light
revelation
star
hill
a man and a woman naked above the grass
the beyond transumptive
shadows of vine leaves
begrudged
gods references
the heavens fields
the man wakened
dream again implicative
foreknowledge the purpose
giant the universal body
total
then to pool
dawn
an angel going down to a valley
odor
radiance
involvement
knowledge
a hill
forsythia
the gift

The man dying the hill flame
the person reflected
people reflecting reflected
then going on
we went up to a wood
rested at the edge
star
field
sea
goat
lion
tiger
deer
insect
sand
cliff
eagle
river
flamingo
particle
desert
grove
sparrow
snow
oak
garden
gull
weed
moon
lake
valley
crystal
dust
words from the self
the pit justifying flame least providential

Angel under willow
fire below by river
road
valley
odor
reduction
the man a reflection
the god involution evolution
resolution deceptive
induction deduction
transformations
therefore equilibration
then opposite
generation
circular movement squared
the confusion
street
river
the failure
flower
foot
the withering
water
bird
branch
hill
grove
mountain
above
beyond
behind
background
the instinct
that
the habit foreground

Inward
the rose
revealing
light
resolving
melody
eagle
revealed
the person
reflecting
the man
on
a
hill
revealing
sea
then
heavens
vast
close
diamond
reflecting
the reduction
lily
then
fire
point
resolution
conic
elliptic
the balance
field
the
flowers
rays

Glass
light
then
hill
rocks
past
beyond
up

Wood
then
up
path
hill right
sea beyond
then
down
rocks
path left
grove
below
hill
valley
between
hill
mountain
valley
then
desert
between
mountain
hill
sea
hill
sea
mountain
resolution
therefore
valley
desert
sea
reduction
wood
self

Spheres ground
air not air spirit
angel moved freely
each planet
different
however
size orbit
apparent
heliocentric
given up to
theocentric
more
less
altering
revealing
differentially relating
equally participating
Reflection
refraction
wake
pool
foot
mountain
wind
one image
tree
river below
wood above
tree reflected
tree reflecting
therefore
light
tree
considering itself
image shade

Seeking to recover the fragrance the hill
we took the path left of a grove
the people below behind the trees
sitting facing the river
our words
dust
in conflict over thought image
the discursive a point in favor of criticism
if intellect imagination were not one
one other to another
other one to itself
persons gathered up
re-defined
the lake defining the man
the suicide
water flow above me
cover me eternally
tense pointless where ground resolution of everywhere
the point rather desire
our wood
our city
light interwoven
river sea
we may never return
the epical falsification
impermanence
humanity split
work leisure
an arrangement
suiting the profiteers
in the wood then dark
light flower word successive transformations
effaced
song vision body face to face
radiating in radiance

Thru mirror in enigma
sea
vision word identity
inner sound darkness
inner vision light
darkness prefiguring light
deafness unsealed
word snow
gravidity
past work returning
not unresolved
rather same word appearance
contingencies
the relation
word finally one
not itself
the dying balanced
the spirit realization
the work the word
unity
full
then the flickering
edge
sea
height
depth
effaced
plain burden
sea universe
crystal
the ethical
meaningless
work word revitalized
signification
vision neither in nor out

moon   skyscrapers
moon   branches

blocked

blue everywhere
light ever
center
unseen
where yes
clearly
flower
not unlike
no

gardens
streets
not wretched
rather
state
projected
discoloring

sit in a park
otherworldly

therefore
to withdraw
from the literary world
is a must
this proves
our style no style
ars imitatur naturam
in sua operatione

it takes courage to go this way
because it is not the way of the world
I mean
the heretics
can no longer be
Luther
Bruno
Campanella
heresy is going against
the Material Ideal
and only the spiritual man can do that
but here going against
is innocuous
no trap
no argument
release
the Material Ideal not something to be destroyed
because the spiritual man not impeded
his movement reaps
enough daily to see thru
release even the Material Ideal

can there be a poetry of pace
no
people
no
no poetry that seeks to release
even the Material Ideal
can be dramatic
epical
or
lyrical
then what kind of poetry is left
given the Hegelian
the Marxist
there can be no poetry
because the upshot is
the Platonic user
maker
no imitator
therefore
the kind of poetry
we postulate
is the kind that resolves
book
canzone
song
what kind is that
theological poetry

on my way back
from my parttime job
I think
have I written malice
because I have failed
to give lip service
to the civil
there are the workers
breaking their backs
the traffic
complements them
I'm the same
only I refuse to submit
my revolt
is not to give in
to any desire
that ultimately leads
to a justification
position achieved
society more fully reformed

then there's the home
I return to my wife and children
their existences
tied up
in the scheme of things
surrounding
how do I alleviate the burdens
I don't
I can't
I'm just a worker
and what is even worse
a poet
who sees his poetry
as work
a means toward an end
do I desire
to be anything other
than a worker
no
thus the tragedy
of my movement
any worker's movement
but the dialectical
is not the thought process
I'm involved in
if involvement
therefore
process
can in no sense
take significance
from a logic
not referable
to application

what about the political situation
it's misleading
of course
it depends upon
your position
in society
how else can you represent
your particular view
no report
can ever claim
to be ubiquitous
therefore
the uselessness
of the reports
they simply reflect
the position's slant
and of course
the Material Ideal
is the better for it
because the solution of
all these slants lies
in the integral
that knows no differences

how far can we go
in our descent
toward particulars
not far
our language
mathematical
or otherwise
just reaps surfaces

it is said that Art is useless
and that if useful
it must be social
and that if not social
then the User Society
cannot be in the position
that dictates

word it again
the imitator is in relation to
Use in the Gift
if this is so
then the notion of audience
takes its significance from
Spirit the spirit an identification
the final identification forgone
therefore
the theological poet
indirectly reveals
the user and maker
in harmonious relation to
the Holy Spirit
because the true object
of the theological poet
is Eternal Form
Species in the Image
the experiential

the senses of the audience
unimpeded
each member released
free to journey his own way
it must be so

the spiritual life is the real
nominalism can take no hold there either
therefore
since the poet's object
is Eternal Form
it follows
that the quieting
of epical desire
is an indication
of the transformation
of the tragic ache
for anterior time
fulfillment real
the tragic way
re-directed
in view of it
it goes without saying
that the comedic resolution
is not total
that's what constitutes
the realism
of the spiritual life

interesting how these same phrases
keep cropping up in my work
over the years
they're the same words
but the significance is different
is this the range of particularization
maybe so
but one thing is sure
God is the reason
and end
of all our movements
we bear witness to the Gift
the fact that work
is not an end in itself
gives us the insight
that our release from it
is not proof
of its uselessness
on the contrary
our release clarifies it
to an extent
that is truly definitive
does this imply
that the self
releases itself from work
only in the end
to look down upon it
that could be read into the release
but it makes no sense
if the release
is Eternal Life
the work Eternal Form
we live in and thru God
therefore
Eternal Form and Eternal Life
are not an identity
Eternal Form
taking its realization from
Spirit the spirit an identification
Use in the Gift

if the spiritual life is fulfillment
then the natural is participative
therefore
a spiritual art is full
altho the fullness
is not due to
the space-time continuum
from this it becomes clear
that the civil
can become like the natural
altho again
not in the sense of
the space-time continuum
because such a perfection
is ontological
an end in itself
which prevents the civil
from releasing itself
from *superbia*
it is true
however
that the civil fulfilled
is no longer the civil
but such a transformation
shows the reality no impediment
therefore
it is clear
how the spiritual artist
can use the natural

the underground is a mania for the particular

a failure
my clothes prove it
my apartment will soon be demolished
yes
renovation

the other circle
circle
no
fulfillment
which
therefore
does away with the word other
draws up the circle
involved in impediment
transforms it
returns it to itself
a circle
no longer in contradiction

behind window
sea
beyond poplars
hill

gull inland
wood right
sun setting

we live no enchanted life
only sea
yesterday
rose
leaves

dragon
sun ray
hold on
kids
wherever gold
blue

the fall of a great house
the body

horses
led
down
hill

stars risen

lying down
resting
not listening
nevertheless
music

no reason to be poetic
but I think
a lot about
our trip to the sea
the place we rented
for $20 a wk
no shower
the bed
pretty bad
room enough for only one

save the political theory
and throw out the rest

or

his work's a cover up
for his lack of experience

ocean
tomb
hearing bird
remembering
standing among trees
no where true
the hills neither behind either
forced back
death the preoccupation
lilacs sensed
cemetery
a boys obsession
the background

the extension of the walls
the senses
the converse
insensible
water
beyond trees
other times
between hill
grove
transformation
preventing
return

we stood on a bridge
the vantage point
a willow
eery

some nights
all we talk about

living outside the city
in a house
above a stream

so I don't know the practical world
I write
for angels

my sense of giving

intelligibles

I can give you no hand
if you wish to kill yourself
go ahead

lie toward the dark
the shade drawn

I'm a white horse
who's
going
to
die

a moment
the world
closed

image
signifies
release

thought
verifies
drawing
up
image

thought never far from image
image drawn up
release

sitting at a back table
in an automat
my glasses off

the window up ahead
setting sun opposite

the jobs
alienate
alienum

where
God
since no one accepts the work
—rest
unaccepted

It is true that my withdrawal from the literary world is complete, but withdrawal can only mean desire of fame (vanity)—writing is not pride: to write for Humanity *God the Subject* alters every sense of the writer as *personality*: therefore, it is not the writer's job to seek out the latest innovations of the day—the principles of craft are perennial; he has ancient teachers, and with them he silently converses.

A wandering seeking new speech entia non sunt multiplicanda praeter necessitatem.

Maybe this is the way it should be: the life empty for all purposes except the poetry that says God the vision everything lived thru not so bad after all: but this is true at the moment of writing; it has no meaning at the moment of living. Such a conflict can't be real; it must be imposed—from where? the outside. Does this exonerate the sufferer?

Words that suggest the country, leisure *despair*—why? because nothing in the life says that I can make it away from the market—my personality has become increasingly withdrawn—can't go anywhere without getting sick—the parties false to my way of thinking, and, of course, that isn't fair—people are entitled to fun, and the gloomy fellow is cancer—he's worth more if he at least knows *to check the feast* is not just.

Here you're just viewing yourself from an occasion belonging to the past—as you say: you're more withdrawn now than ever; and this is a sickness; however, the sense that seems to irk you most is that you still have a long way to go—if you were 60, you could breathe easier: at last it's over! but not yet 40, the spirit balks, doesn't have the strength to renew if withdrawal is acute.

The quiet I can't achieve comes to me at work only as a phrase. I may pause, look up from my desk toward windows fronting similar buildings, knowing that the freedom that supposedly belongs to the pedestrians has me as an onlooker, the secure position more secure behind bars.

The man moves, the angel illuminates, full common society the ground the Holy Spirit the foundation the Way toward final release.

I am a slave seeking a corner at night to write.

Should a writer gossip about his personal life?
autobiography
modern
false

kids
bounding
down
from
rocks
hit
the
shore
forcefully
and
then
run
the
length
o f
it

walking thru woods
coming upon lilies
the past life
a lake
          haunting

from above
under a tree
people huddled close
gloating over
a man losing his footing
grasping a ledge
unable to hold on
letting go

people
objects
the public square
infinite
space

I go up a hill and sit with my
children on a rock

the tree below quiet more

center

I lived daily the spiritual
my meals taken alone
the reality false
the position
never ubiquitous
went to a coffee shop
the discussions
war
city
one said
war national
the other
city familial
both
therefore
nation
home
complement
other talk
folk singers approximate realities better
we are at the beginnings again
then the position of onlooker
uninvolved
not choice but birth
the language becoming less visional
yet at a certain level
whatever the word
the total vision reflective
then going on
reason
a loss
the spirit cut off
Spirit seeking the spirit
in grass love
light going

The future then and a death
arrived late
somewhere
near midnight
took the only rooms available
the horizon
sea
light as far as the door
the
shade
less
than
half
way
drawn
startled
went to the window
a
group
o f
people
up
from
the
beach
outside
the
bar
across
the
street
turned away
the painting above the bed
a storm
ship going under

a park poet ok a bum

intuiting farthest light
standing in a grove
on a hillside
a man conveyed rays
to an angel below
facing sea
reflecting only
gull

ocean liner
gone behind
cliffs

the wake
however
still

glimmering

in passing

old doors
at the edge
of a lot

dying then
in the wave's
intenser
day

in contrast to the bright
day a junk shop and an
old lady in a rocker

to vanish is to release
the world

shadows of weeds on a rock
evening returning

object
      to
           object

Lumen Gloriae (1973)

FROM *INFINITESMALS*

I sit in a house
literally
falling about
my ears

the courts
weigh
the issues

deem
pros and cons
necessary

in poverty
    knowing nobody
water flowing in
    from all sides

riding a train

looking at homes

desiring a home

poor drunk
asleep on the sidewalk
clutching his penis

ashes

even so

odor

essence

an old man leaning out of a window
knowing himself useless
          the potted plant beside him
backing it up

going down to the river
I look across to the hills
my spirit in union
triumph over opposites

pigeons

all

in a flash

under one

tree

a whole garden of angels
each leaning upon each
light flowering heavenward
tho each flower heaven
animals under flame
key releasing ground
fire air earth water
outside the walls

leaving the airport
taking the bus
riding past cemetery
thru shopping district
the city truer
                dustier
the guest gone

shucking our bathing suits

the little window
above the sink
blinding

after supper in chinatown
we walked home along the Bowery
our attention
quickened by a crash
somebody put a rock
or something or other
thru a shop window
then ran up the stairs
of the hotel
a few doors down

ghostly
petals
whirling
about

offsetting
shaded
walk

haunt
even
waking
dream

when I got off the bus there she was
I hadnt seen her for almost 3 wks
we walked up a ways to the cottage

moonlight in the room
our bodies exhausted from loving
we lay talking
sleep surprising

a couple on a bench
their kids over
by the sand pile
even tho rain
any minute

curving the road
                    overlooking
a lake

other cars
             alongside
contributing

to
   the
symmetry

longing for purity
finding oneself
instead
a wanderer
amidst
      at the edge of
green

no greater vista
than the inward
opening

       out

           and beyond

vacationers by the hundreds
climbed the sand dunes
and then at intervals
ran down recklessly
what seemed like steps

in a clearing
in a wood
at twilight
a family

walking about
gathering
strange enough
driftwood

a turn around the city
but if the streets
show degeneration
then no cruise
can alter that fact
despite the guide
speaking directly
to the out-of-towners
and the foreigners

Then the dwelling of the angel in the soul
or rather the odor
sign
of the dwelling
continuing
habituating the man
to the daily
drawing out radiance
preparing
rendering
transparent
the surroundings
the universe
the aureole
receiving
truest
ray

body in grass
elliptically formed
in turn inscribed
in square
in flame
flower
center
sustained
by
four
angels

FROM *DISIGILLA*

from the distance of a return home
an evocation of a walk thru the city
the flow of people characteristic
the pilgrim secure upon the waters

proving ground

they came to the eastside
making their mark

scattering afterwards
buying farms or cottages

while one or two others maybe
unknown to each other
continue to roam city

finding out a generation later
old news
a newspaper partly in slush

at the foot
of a block
of turn-of-the-century
tenements

a great bridge
leading up
or falling off
to nowhere

love	knowledge	divided
mysticism	science	divided
union	identity	divided
glorified body	spiritual man	undivided

the heart skips a beat
when the sun withdraws

something like a fall

an elevator from the 15th
to the 1st
without a stop

duality is rhythm   the essence of duality is rhythm

the essence or nature of rhythm is duality
positive and negative poles alternating indefinitely
the inner structure indefinite total combination

from Letargo (1980)

forest dweller
a mirror

snow rain fall
sun recovers day

the jar broken
at his feet

I descend
from room
to street
to walk

the realities
that float
and sink—

lily
in hand
I ascend
from odor
to odor

my art
the arc

not practice

seaweed!

float thru
&
    beyond—

a walk
you
      might

say

or
a
   sleep

only
sans

city

give over, then, go daily

tired of the world,
creation also
seems far
fetched:

    voice
voiceless speaking
not the
same

nightly
I sit up
in my high
tower
not given
over
onto field
or hill
but onto rows
and rows
of babylonian
windows
and down
I go
in
my
wizardry
di
ur
nal
ly

Poet not poet no longer Poet

his eye the negation of division itself

the eyes not aquila

                                    his
voice not his own either, coming as it did
thrice removed upon any and every voicing

there was odor
he was garden
seraphs dwelt in him
he responded in grace
he branch
finally light
in itself

from Manifestatio (1991)

some rooms have the feel
of outside in

she met him at a bar

later on she told him
she tried
eyeing him
for the longest
time

no go
he just sat
so sad
head hanging
at the bar

then after he left
she figured
maybe he'd
stop at
the bar
down the street

he bought her a drink
with his last dollar

they kissed in the booth
her hotel room
a joint
but when he woke
before dawn
the surprise
still here
she hadn't asked him
to leave

they ate supper
scrambled eggs
and toast
at a luncheonette
she paid the bill

they talked
finding out   about
each other

it didn't much matter
to her

he stayed at home
studying Aquinas

sometimes
                    before
entering
the apartment
she'd pause
at the door
eternal
             as
the evening light
across
             his
                    open
book

even so
                they continued
going
to
        the
                bar

usually leaving
at four a.m.

stopping off
at a hole
in the wall
for a bite

then home

making love

the birds metallic

the springs
of the
hideaway

singing

longed for

new moon
tho full
only a
day after

a period
of return

a young couple
to each other
always close
shy
      of

           any

eye

from 1991 Circolazione

Looking at the in

        the music within

my childhood

        in communion white

very Italian

    in America

On in age, face is everything
I love your face
bird in open grass
sitting on the springs of a lounge
against wall, watching
water in bed, then
when drinking

in seconds

If I stare from room to screen
to window to branch

a light comes to me a wanderer

                          my weariness
not even able to get up,

                    enlightened